Oceans

Joy Palmer

Watts Books
London • New York • Sydney

© Watts Books 1991
Paperback edition 1995

Watts Books
96 Leonard Street
London EC2A 4RH

Franklin Watts Australia
14 Mars Road
Lane Cove
NSW 2066

ISBN: 0 7496 0572 3 (hardback)
ISBN: 0 7496 2319 5 (paperback)

10 9 8 7 6 5 4 3 2 1

Editor: A. Patricia Sechi
Designer: Shaun Barlow
Cover Design: K and Co
Artwork: Alex Pang
Cover Artwork: Hayward Art Group

Educational Advisor: Joy Richardson
Consultant: Miranda MacQuitty

A CIP catalogue record for this book
is available from the British Library

Printed in Italy
by G. Canale & Co. SpA

Contents

What are oceans?

Most of the earth is covered in water. You can look at a globe to see how much of the earth's surface is coloured blue. This water lies around the land and each large area is called an ocean. Thousands of different plants and animals live in the oceans.

▽ Oceans cover large areas of the earth. They stretch for thousands of kilometres.

Where are oceans?

There are four oceans called the Pacific, the Atlantic, the Indian and the Arctic. The Pacific is the largest ocean. It covers more of the earth's surface than all the land put together!

The oceans contain smaller areas of water called **seas**. Land shapes partly cut these off from the oceans.

▽ Beaches are sometimes made where the oceans meet the land.

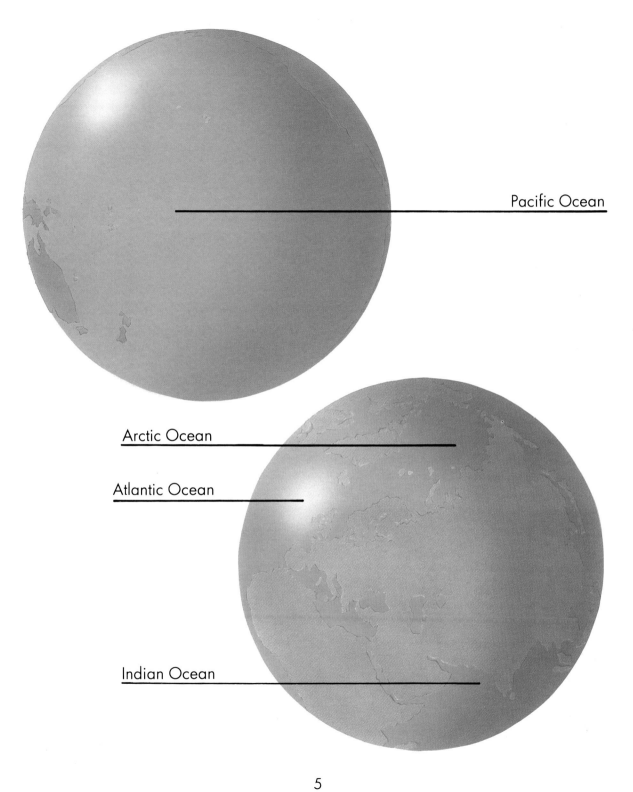

Pacific Ocean

Arctic Ocean

Atlantic Ocean

Indian Ocean

What are oceans like?

If you watch the ocean for a day, you can see the water level rise and fall, as the **tide** goes in and out. The tides are made by the pull of the sun and moon on the earth.

Seawater is salty because it contains **minerals**. They come from rocks which are worn away and washed into the sea.

▷ Salt in seawater dries in the sun and leaves white crystals.

▽ At low tide the sea-level falls. It may be so low it leaves the seabed showing.

▽ At high tide the sea-level rises.

Are oceans warm or cold?

Near the **equator,** the oceans are warm. Near the North and South Poles, the oceans are so cold that the surface freezes.

The movement of the waves carries warm or cold water to different parts of the oceans. The ocean usually becomes colder, the deeper it becomes.

▷ Warm clear seas sometimes have shallow water where many small animals live.

▽ Huge icebergs float in the sea at the South Pole.

Waves

The water in the world's oceans is never still. The wind makes ripples and waves. If the wind blows hard for a long time, the waves grow bigger and stronger. Sometimes the earth moves under the sea. This can set off a huge tidal wave. When tidal waves reach land their force can kill people and destroy homes.

▷ Tidal waves are huge waves. They are very dangerous.

▽ A slight wind makes small waves called ripples.

▽ Waves can wear away land leaving strangely shaped cliffs and rocks.

▽ Waves which break up are called whitecaps.

Plants

Plants which live in the oceans have to be able to survive the salt. Many seaweeds live in the oceans. They do not live in deep water as they need sunlight to survive. Land plants are stiff, but water plants are bendy so they can move in the water and do not snap. Near the shore, plants grow in marshes and on the sand.

▽ Cord grass grows in marshes. It gets rid of the salt it takes in by sweating it out.

▽ Mangrove trees grow in swamps. Their large roots stop them from being washed away.

▽ Eelgrass is not a seaweed, but it is a plant which grows in the sea.

△ Many seaweeds have air-filled pockets which keep them afloat near the light.

▽ Some seaweeds are red or brown.

Fish

Fish live in all the oceans. Their bodies are smooth and tapering to move easily through the water. They breathe through **gills** which take in air from the water.

   Fish live at different levels of the oceans. The lantern fish lives deep down and sardines live near the surface. Most fish eat smaller fish to survive.

▷Many smaller fish live in groups or shoals to protect themselves against enemies.

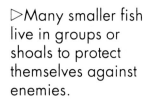

△ Tuna fish live in all the oceans except the coldest.

△ Rays are flat fish which live on the sea bed.

◁ The shape of a shark's body helps it move quickly through the ocean.

◁ Sardines are small fish which live in groups, near the surface of the ocean.

▽ The lantern fish glows green to draw other fish near, which it catches.

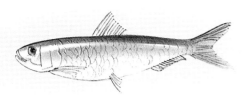

△ The plaice's colour hides it from other fish which may want to eat it.

Fantastic creatures

There are many strange looking creatures living in the oceans like the octopus and the jellyfish. Each animal is suited to the part of the ocean where it lives. Sea anemones stay in the same spot. Crabs crawl along the sea bottom where they catch their food.

▽ The seahorse is a fish. It lives amongst seaweeds and underwater grasses.

▷ Jellyfish are bell-shaped and have many tentacles or arms.

▽ Anemones sting animals with their many arms and then eat them.

▽ The octopus lives on the sea bed. It uses its arms to catch passing animals.

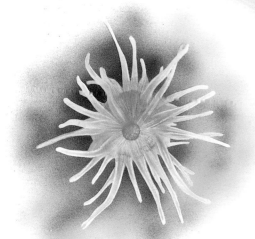

▽ Crabs use their large pincers to hold food.

△ Starfish live in deep water. They eat shellfish and crabs.

▽ Tiny creatures and plants called plankton live in seawater.

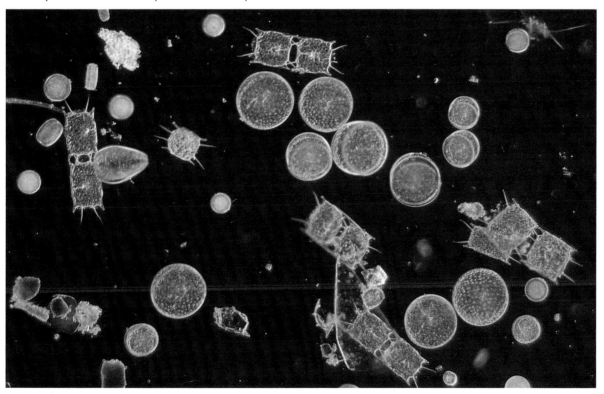

Mammals and reptiles

Whales are the largest creatures in the sea. Whales look like fish, but they are **mammals**. Like us, they have lungs and cannot stay under water all the time. They come to the surface to breathe.

Sea snakes and turtles are **reptiles** which live in the sea. Reptiles breathe air and have scaly skins.

▽ The sea otter is a furry creature. It eats shellfish and crabs while floating.

▽ Seals are mammals. Some live close to the land, but others live out at sea.

▷ The sea snake has a paddle-shaped tail to help it swim.

▷ The killer whale is easy to spot because of its black and white markings.

▽ The shape of a dolphin's body lets it move quickly through the water.

▷ The green turtle lives in the warm oceans of the world.

Birds

Sea birds live on land near the oceans. They rely on the seas for food. Many sea birds have webbed feet and well-oiled feathers. Birds, such as gulls and pelicans usually stay close to the land. Penguins spend most of their lives at sea.

▽ The albatross has the largest wingspan of all sea birds.

△ Sailors know they are near land when they see gulls flying above.

◁ Puffins live near the shore and on islands in the northern oceans.

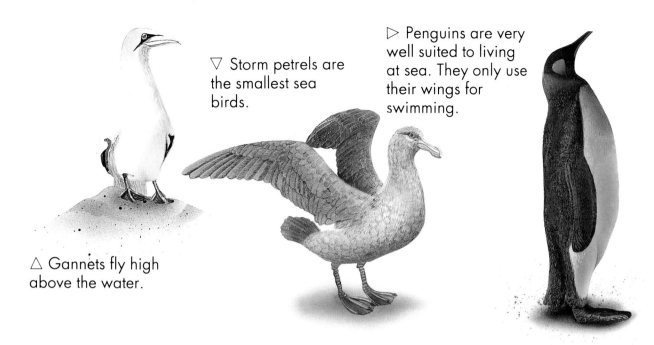

▽ Storm petrels are the smallest sea birds.

▷ Penguins are very well suited to living at sea. They only use their wings for swimming.

△ Gannets fly high above the water.

▽ The brown pelican is a sea bird. Other pelicans live near fresh water.

People and the ocean

Sometimes we only see the world's oceans when we go on holiday. Here we can go swimming and sailing. People work on the oceans in fishing boats or on oil platforms. We use the seas like roads too. For thousands of years people have travelled across the seas carrying goods from country to country.

▷ In some countries seaweed is farmed for food.

▽ Many people go sailing in small boats.

▷ Windsurfing is a popular sport. Many windsurfers are seen near beaches.

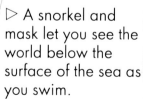

▷ A snorkel and mask let you see the world below the surface of the sea as you swim.

▽ Oil is drilled from the sea bed and pumped ashore.

◁ Large ships called tankers carry oil across the oceans.

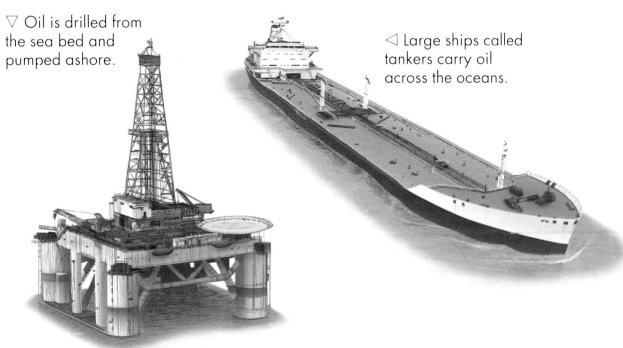

Riches from the seas

The oceans give us food, energy and minerals. Millions of fish are caught each year for eating. Fish is also used to make oil or animal feed. Power from the ocean waves is used to make electricity in some countries. We gather salt from the sea. And we use coral and pearls in jewellery.

▽ Salt is gathered from pans where seawater has dried out.

▽ Sponges are the skeletons of sea creatures.

◁ Coral is a mass of tubes made for shelter by tiny animals. It is made into jewellery.

▷ This power station makes electricity from the rise and fall of the waves.

▽ Pearls are found in shellfish called oysters. Pearls are like small beads.

▽ Fishing boats catch fish by using large nets or pumps.

Threats to the oceans

We use the sea, but we must learn to protect it. Some fish will die out if we do not cut down the numbers caught each year. Visitors leave litter behind. It may harm animals which become caught in plastic wrappings. Waste is dumped at sea, **polluting** the water and killing animals.

▷ Oil spills kill many sea animals which swallow the oil or become coated in it.

▽ Overfishing reduces the numbers of fish and some kinds could die out altogether.

▷ Litter spoils beaches and can be dangerous.

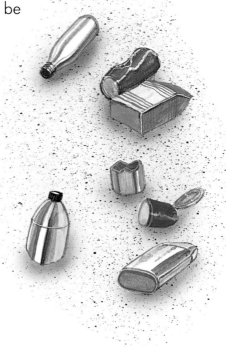

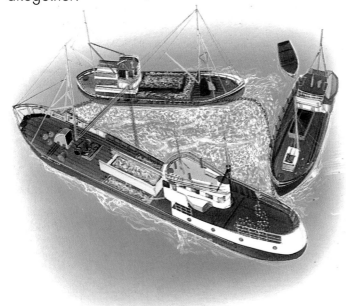

▽ Factories dump waste chemicals into the sea.

Ocean dangers

Safety at sea is important. Many people who go sailing wear lifejackets in case they fall overboard. Lighthouses warn sailors of rocks. Lightbuoys mark where ships can sail safely. If a boat is in trouble at sea, lifeboats are sent out. On the beach, lifeguards keep a watch for people who may need help.

▽ A lighthouse has a light which can be seen far out to sea to warn ships of danger.

△ This lifejacket is an inflatable vest which keeps you afloat.

◁ Lifeguards keep watch on the shore for people who may be drowning.

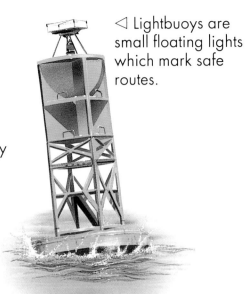

◁ Lightbuoys are small floating lights which mark safe routes.

▽ Lifeboats are launched to rescue people in trouble at sea.

Things to do

- When you visit the seashore, collect the shells of sea creatures. Only collect the shells if there is no creature inside

- Collect pebbles or pieces of wood from the beach. Look to see how the waves have shaped and smoothed them.

- Look through a magnifying glass at a handful of sand. What can you find? You may be able to see bits of shell and rock. What colour are they?

Useful addresses:

Greenpeace Ltd.
30 Islington Road
London N1

Marine Conservation Society
4 Gloucester Road
Ross-on-Wye HR9 5BU

Worldwide Fund for Nature
Panda House
11-13 Ockford Road
Godalming
Surrey GU7 1QU

Glossary

beach A strip of land at the edge of the sea, created by the waves leaving behind rocks and shells they are carrying.

cliffs High, steep rocks which drop into the sea.

equator The equator is an imaginary line around the middle of the earth.

gills Comb-like structures which fish use to absorb oxygen from the water to breathe.

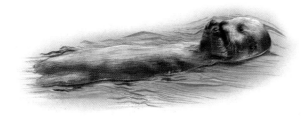

mammal An animal which has hair, gives birth to its young and feeds them with milk.

mineral A mineral is any substance, which is not alive, which can be dug out of the ground. Coal, gold and diamonds are minerals.

plankton Microscopic animals and plants which live in the oceans.

pollution Spoiling the oceans, land and air by dumping wastes and other harmful substances.

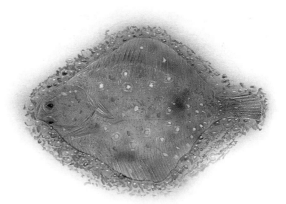

predator An animal which kills and eats other animals.

reptile An animal which has a scaly skin and which lays eggs, such as snakes or lizards.

sea The water in all the oceans which is salty. An area of ocean which is partly surrounded by land.

tide The rise and fall of the sea each day. It is caused by the pull of the moon and the sun on the earth.

Index

Photographic credits: Bruce Coleman 23, (C B & D W Frith) 9, (Dr Eckart Pott) 13, 21, (Bill Wood) 15; Robert Harding 29, (David Lomax) 25; Eric and David Hosking (D P Wilson) 17; Frank Lane Picture Agency 4; NHPA (David Woodfall) 27; Survival Anglia (Dieter and Mary Plage) 11; Zefa 3.